The Super Fab Financial Planner

© 2015 Tonya Rapley

First Edition

Designed by Kaye McCoy of 7th Street Studio, LLC.

ISBN- 978-1517532840

All rights reserved. No part of this book may be reproduced, scanned, or distributed in any printed or electronic form without permission.

The Not Just For Profit, LLC

www.myfabfinance.com

WELCOME

Our busy lives make it easy for tasks to go undone and paperwork to become disorganized; before we know it disorganization induced paralysis can quickly set in. This lack of organization can prevent you from achieving your goals, whether personal or financial. For that reason I created the Super Fab Finance planner.

My goal with this planner is to help you gain clarity around your situation, declutter your finances, and structure your financial freedom plan accordingly.

The Super Fab Finance Planner originates from the successful My Fab Finance Financial printables which were downloaded by over 5,000 MyFabFinance.com readers. After a year and a half of distribution and brutally honest feedback, My Fab Finance readers spoke. They wanted an actual workbook that didn't require monthly printing, one that kept the pages all in one place.

I listened. So...here we are.

My ultimate goal is to create tools that empower individuals to lead fabulous and financially responsible lives. I hope that you find this planner as useful as I intend it to be.

If you have questions about how to use this workbook or want to rave about it to the world, please use the hashtag *#SuperFabFinance.* Let others know that you have decided to commit to your financial excellence!

Thank you again for purchasing this Super Fab Financial Planner.
I appreciate you more than words could express.

Love,
Tonya

HOW TO USE THIS PLANNER

If you are unsure of how to use any of the worksheets in this book this page provides an overview on how to use each page to ensure that you get the most out of your purchase and most importantly, successfully organize your finances.

Certain pages are customizable so that no matter when the workbook is ordered, it will be relevant.

MONTHLY BUDGET (Monthly) - The budget worksheet is pre-filled with the most common items in a house- hold budget. Enter the estimated amount you regularly spend or would like to regularly spend in the Budget column. Enter the amount you actually spent in the Actual column. Once the month is over subtract the different of these two to see where you went over or under budget. Everyone's financial situation is different. If something doesn't apply to you, cross it out and replace it with something that does or leave it blank altogether.

GRATITUDE JOURNAL (Monthly) - At the beginning of each month think about what you are grateful for and write it out on this page. Try not to repeat yourself and challenge yourself to recognize the know and unknown blessings in your life Whenever you are feeling a bit down, go back read your previous entries for a reminder of everything you have to be thankful for.

FINANCIAL CALENDAR (Monthly) - Customize the calendars by filling in the dates for the month you are in. Use the space available for each date to record your utility, credit card, loan due dates or any other important events that could potentially impact your finances such as doctor's appointments, membership dues, etc.

ACCOUNT INFORMATION (Months 1,6,12) - Use this worksheet to store commonly used account information such as insurance, bank accounts, savings accounts, online trading accounts, etc.

DEBT REPAYMENT (Months 1,4,7,10) - Determine your debt amounts and plan your repayment schedule. Use a separate page for each account. Not only can you keep track of your payment amount and balances but top section contains important details that you may be too busy to keep track of, such as interest rates, phone numbers, etc.

DAILY EXPENSE TRACKER (Monthly) - This is a spending log. The purchases are broken down into categories so that you can see how many of your purchases are needs versus wants. After a week or longer I encourage you to reflect on your spending habits and determine where you are spending excessively.

NETWORTH BALANCE (Months 1,6,12) - This sheet provides a snapshot of your finances by tracking all your assets and liabilities. Remember: Your assets are what you own and your liabilities are what you owe others. When you subtract the total of these two that is your networth. You will do this assessment twice in the book, once at the beginning and once at the end to chart your progress.

TRANSITION PAGE (Monthly) - These pages are indicators that a new month of pages are starting. On these pages you will find an inspirational quote or reminder, along with a fun, monthly financial challenge and a to-do list. On this to-do list record any financial goals you would like to accomplish for that month.

Have more questions? No problem.
Ask via social media using the *#SuperFabFinance* hashtag or at *www.myfabfinance.com*

GOALS

Before we get started answer the following questions.

WHAT DO I WANT IN LIFE?
Think about things that make you happy on a deep, lasting level.

_____

_____

_____

_____

WHAT DO I **NOT** WANT IN LIFE?
Think about things that create blocks, take up time, cause stress and/or aren't appropriately supporting you.

_____

_____

_____

_____

MY TOP 3 PRIORITIES IN LIFE:

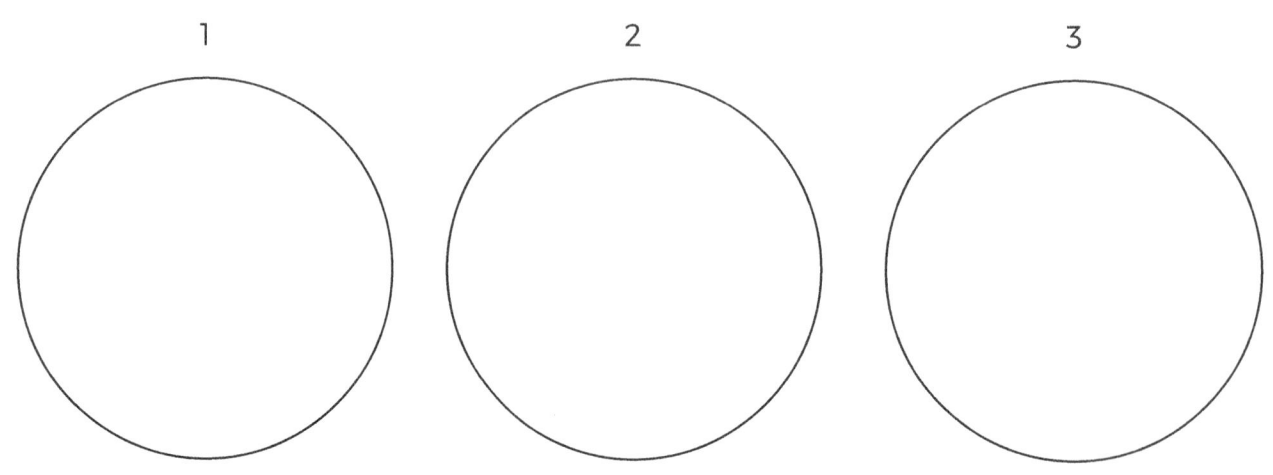

DESIGN YOUR LIFE

Describe your ideal life 10 years from now.

Think about:
- What you want to be doing for a living
- Where you want to live
- The types of relationships you want to have
- Where you would like to travel
- How you want to feel

Don't limit yourself here.
Shamelessly explore your wildest dreams and write down what comes to mind.

_____

_____

_____

_____

_____

_____

_____

_____

_____

_____

_____

MONTH 1

HONESTY AND ACKNOWLEDGMENT OF THE STATE OF YOUR CURRENT SITUATION IS THE FIRST STEP TO CHANGING YOUR SITUATION.

MONTHLY CHALLENGE:

Reduce your monthly bills.

Assess your monthly bills and find a way to reduce the cost of at least one of them.

GOALS FOR THIS MONTH:

○
○
○

I'M GRATEFUL FOR

TALK MONEY WITH TONYA

FINANCIAL BOUNDARIES

One time or another, we all have to think about creating financial boundaries. By setting financial boundaries, you do not only preserve and protect your financial future, but the financial future of those who depend on you. When you allow yourself to become someone's saving account you aren't being fair to yourself nor honoring your goals.

There are times where I have loaned and/or have given money to family and friends; but I only give it when I have it to give. If you are going to miss a payment or a deposit into your savings account because you loaned money, that means you don't have it to give.

If you're not taking care of your finances, insuring that all of your needs are met and goals are being accomplished, then it will be hard for you to be of benefit to someone down the line. Sometimes it can be difficult to tell a family member or a friend "no," but I challenge you to think about the bigger picture. Think about how saying "no" at this moment will allow you to say "yes" in the future when they need you the most.

FINANCIAL CALENDAR

MONDAY	TUESDAY	WEDNESDAY	THURSDAY	FRIDAY	SATURDAY	SUNDAY

MYFABFINANCE.COM

MONTHLY BUDGET

INCOME	BUDGET	ACTUAL	DIFFERENCE	NOTES
SOURCE	$			
SOURCE	$			
TOTAL	$			
SAVINGS				
TOTAL	$			
INVESTING/RETIREMENTS				
	$			
	$			
TOTAL	$			
HOUSING + UTILITIES				
	$			
	$			
	$			
	$			
TOTAL	$			
STUDENT LOANS				
	$			
	$			
TOTAL	$			
TRANSPORTATION				
CAR PAYMENTS	$			
PUBLIC TRANSPORTATION	$			
TAXI	$			
INSURANCE	$			
GAS	$			
TOTAL	$			
FOOD				
GROCERIES	$			
DINING OUT	$			
TOTAL	$			
PERSONAL				
TOILETRIES	$			
BEAUTY (HAIR & NAILS)	$			
OTHER	$			
MEDICAL	$			
TOTAL	$			
CREDIT CARDS				
	$			
	$			
	$			
TOTAL	$			
OTHER EXPENSES				
	$			
	$			
	$			
TOTAL	$			
GRAND TOTAL	$			

DAILY EXPENSE TRACKER

DATE	DESCRIPTION	CATEGORY	AMOUNT	CASH/ CREDIT OR DEBIT?	NEED OR WANT?
			$		
			$		
			$		
			$		
			$		
			$		
			$		
			$		
			$		
			$		
			$		
			$		
			$		
			$		
			$		
			$		
			$		
			$		
			$		
			$		
			$		
			$		
			$		
			$		
			$		
		TOTAL	$		

MYFABFINANCE.COM

DEBT REPAYMENT PLAN

COMPANY INFO		ACCOUNT NUMBER	CREDIT TYPE
CREDIT LIMIT	INTEREST RATE	TERM	INTEREST ACCRUED
GOAL PAYOFF DATE	MINIMUM PAYMENT	DUE DATE	STARTING BALANCE
WEBSITE		USERNAME	PASSWORD

BALANCE	PAYMENT AMOUNT	DATE	CURRENT AMOUNT	NOTES

MYFABFINANCE.COM

DEBT REPAYMENT PLAN

COMPANY INFO		ACCOUNT NUMBER	CREDIT TYPE
CREDIT LIMIT	INTEREST RATE	TERM	INTEREST ACCRUED
GOAL PAYOFF DATE	MINIMUM PAYMENT	DUE DATE	STARTING BALANCE
WEBSITE		USERNAME	PASSWORD

BALANCE	PAYMENT AMOUNT	DATE	CURRENT AMOUNT	NOTES

MYFABFINANCE.COM

DEBT REPAYMENT PLAN

COMPANY INFO		ACCOUNT NUMBER	CREDIT TYPE
CREDIT LIMIT	INTEREST RATE	TERM	INTEREST ACCRUED
GOAL PAYOFF DATE	MINIMUM PAYMENT	DUE DATE	STARTING BALANCE
WEBSITE		USERNAME	PASSWORD

BALANCE	PAYMENT AMOUNT	DATE	CURRENT AMOUNT	NOTES

NETWORTH BALANCE

ASSETS			LIABILITIES		
CASH			**DEBTS**		
		$			$
		$			$
		$			$
		$			$
		$			$
	SUBTOTAL	$		SUBTOTAL	$
REAL ESTATE			**MORTGAGES**		
		$			$
		$			$
		$			$
		$			$
		$			$
	SUBTOTAL	$		SUBTOTAL	$
INVESTMENTS			**LOANS**		
		$			$
		$			$
		$			$
		$			$
		$			$
	SUBTOTAL	$		SUBTOTAL	$
	TOTAL	$		**TOTAL**	$

DATE	TOTAL ASSETS	TOTAL LIABILITY	NETWORTH

FICO SCORE	EQUIFAX	EXPIRIAN	TRANS UNION

MYFABFINANCE.COM

ACCOUNT INFORMATION

COMPANY INFO		ACCOUNT NUMBER
WEBSITE		SECURITY QUESTION
USERNAME	PASSWORD	SECURITY ANSWER
COMPANY INFO		ACCOUNT NUMBER
WEBSITE		SECURITY QUESTION
USERNAME	PASSWORD	SECURITY ANSWER
COMPANY INFO		ACCOUNT NUMBER
WEBSITE		SECURITY QUESTION
USERNAME	PASSWORD	SECURITY ANSWER
COMPANY INFO		ACCOUNT NUMBER
WEBSITE		SECURITY QUESTION
USERNAME	PASSWORD	SECURITY ANSWER
COMPANY INFO		ACCOUNT NUMBER
WEBSITE		SECURITY QUESTION
USERNAME	PASSWORD	SECURITY ANSWER
COMPANY INFO		ACCOUNT NUMBER
WEBSITE		SECURITY QUESTION
USERNAME	PASSWORD	SECURITY ANSWER

MYFABFINANCE.COM

ACCOUNT INFORMATION

COMPANY INFO		ACCOUNT NUMBER
WEBSITE		SECURITY QUESTION
USERNAME	PASSWORD	SECURITY ANSWER
COMPANY INFO		ACCOUNT NUMBER
WEBSITE		SECURITY QUESTION
USERNAME	PASSWORD	SECURITY ANSWER
COMPANY INFO		ACCOUNT NUMBER
WEBSITE		SECURITY QUESTION
USERNAME	PASSWORD	SECURITY ANSWER
COMPANY INFO		ACCOUNT NUMBER
WEBSITE		SECURITY QUESTION
USERNAME	PASSWORD	SECURITY ANSWER
COMPANY INFO		ACCOUNT NUMBER
WEBSITE		SECURITY QUESTION
USERNAME	PASSWORD	SECURITY ANSWER
COMPANY INFO		ACCOUNT NUMBER
WEBSITE		SECURITY QUESTION
USERNAME	PASSWORD	SECURITY ANSWER

MYFABFINANCE.COM

MONTH 2

"IT'S NOT WHAT YOU *EARN* THAT MAKES YOU WEALTHY, IT'S WHAT YOU *KEEP*"

MONTHLY CHALLENGE:

Check your bank account balance every morning for 30 days (text alerts do not count.)

Checking your primary bank account balance helps you monitor your spending and fraudulent transactions.

GOALS FOR THIS MONTH:

○

○

○

MYFABFINANCE.COM

I'M GRATEFUL FOR

FINANCIAL CALENDAR

MONTH OF: _____

MONDAY	TUESDAY	WEDNESDAY	THURSDAY	FRIDAY	SATURDAY	SUNDAY

MONTHLY BUDGET

INCOME	BUDGET	ACTUAL	DIFFERENCE	NOTES
SOURCE	$			
SOURCE	$			
TOTAL	$			
SAVINGS				
TOTAL	$			
INVESTING/RETIREMENTS				
	$			
	$			
TOTAL	$			
HOUSING + UTILITIES				
	$			
	$			
	$			
	$			
TOTAL	$			
STUDENT LOANS				
	$			
	$			
TOTAL	$			
TRANSPORTATION				
CAR PAYMENTS	$			
PUBLIC TRANSPORTATION	$			
TAXI	$			
INSURANCE	$			
GAS	$			
TOTAL	$			
FOOD				
GROCERIES	$			
DINING OUT	$			
TOTAL	$			
PERSONAL				
TOILETRIES	$			
BEAUTY (HAIR & NAILS)	$			
OTHER	$			
MEDICAL	$			
TOTAL	$			
CREDIT CARDS				
	$			
	$			
	$			
TOTAL	$			
OTHER EXPENSES				
	$			
	$			
	$			
TOTAL	$			
GRAND TOTAL	$			

DAILY EXPENSE TRACKER

DATE	DESCRIPTION	CATEGORY	AMOUNT	CASH/ CREDIT OR DEBIT?	NEED OR WANT?
			$		
			$		
			$		
			$		
			$		
			$		
			$		
			$		
			$		
			$		
			$		
			$		
			$		
			$		
			$		
			$		
			$		
			$		
			$		
			$		
			$		
			$		
			$		
			$		
			$		
			$		
		TOTAL	$		

MYFABFINANCE.COM

MONTH 3

> *"THERE'S A DIFFERENCE BETWEEN COMMON SENSE AND COMMON PRACTICE. YOU CAN HAVE ALL OF THE KNOWLEDGE IN THE WORLD, BUT IF YOU DON'T APPLY IT, IT'S USELESS."*

MONTHLY CHALLENGE:

30 Day No-Shopping Spree

Go 30 days without shopping for clothes (and try to stretch it to 60, 90, 120 days).

GOALS FOR THIS MONTH:

- ○
- ○
- ○

MYFABFINANCE.COM

I'M GRATEFUL FOR

TALK MONEY WITH TONYA

IMPULSE BUYS

Impulse buys are the bane of your budget's existence. You can end up throwing your entire budget and all your financial achievements out the window with a single swipe of a card. However, all hope is not lost. Instead of throwing a pity party when you overspend, take time to reflect and come up with solutions to prevent it from happening again (and return any merchandise if you can).

HERE ARE A FOUR EFFECTIVE WAYS TO CURB IMPULSE SPENDING:

1. Stop going into stores or online store. After all, it's pretty hard to buy things when you aren't going to places where things are sold.

2. Go shopping with lists and challenge yourself to only buy what's on the list.

3. Leave your cards at home and remove auto-pay features from your favorite online stores. It's an oldie but goody that really works. If you do happen to stumble into a store you won't have your credit cards to fall back on.

4. Before making an impulse purchase, ask yourself how the purchase of xyz item will affect your financial goals. At the end of the day remember, you tell your money where to go, it doesn't tell you. You have the power.

MONTH OF: _____

FINANCIAL CALENDAR

MONDAY	TUESDAY	WEDNESDAY	THURSDAY	FRIDAY	SATURDAY	SUNDAY

MYFABFINANCE.COM

MONTHLY BUDGET

INCOME	BUDGET	ACTUAL	DIFFERENCE	NOTES
SOURCE	$			
SOURCE	$			
TOTAL	$			
SAVINGS				
TOTAL	$			
INVESTING/RETIREMENTS				
	$			
	$			
TOTAL	$			
HOUSING + UTILITIES				
	$			
	$			
	$			
	$			
TOTAL	$			
STUDENT LOANS				
	$			
	$			
TOTAL	$			
TRANSPORTATION				
CAR PAYMENTS	$			
PUBLIC TRANSPORTATION	$			
TAXI	$			
INSURANCE	$			
GAS	$			
TOTAL	$			
FOOD				
GROCERIES	$			
DINING OUT	$			
TOTAL	$			
PERSONAL				
TOILETRIES	$			
BEAUTY (HAIR & NAILS)	$			
OTHER	$			
MEDICAL	$			
TOTAL	$			
CREDIT CARDS				
	$			
	$			
	$			
TOTAL	$			
OTHER EXPENSES				
	$			
	$			
	$			
TOTAL	$			
GRAND TOTAL	$			

DAILY EXPENSE TRACKER

DATE	DESCRIPTION	CATEGORY	AMOUNT	CASH/ CREDIT OR DEBIT?	NEED OR WANT?
			$		
			$		
			$		
			$		
			$		
			$		
			$		
			$		
			$		
			$		
			$		
			$		
			$		
			$		
			$		
			$		
			$		
			$		
			$		
			$		
			$		
			$		
			$		
			$		
		TOTAL	$		

MYFABFINANCE.COM

MONTH 4

> *"INVESTING IN YOURSELF IS ONE OF THE BEST INVESTMENTS YOU CAN MAKE"*

MONTHLY CHALLENGE:

Learn a new financial lesson each week.

Suggested topics include: Mutual Funds, IRA's, compound interest, Life Insurance, Estate Planning, Stocks and Bonds

GOALS FOR THIS MONTH:

○
○
○

I'M GRATEFUL FOR

FINANCIAL CALENDAR

MONDAY	TUESDAY	WEDNESDAY	THURSDAY	FRIDAY	SATURDAY	SUNDAY

MYFABFINANCE.COM

MONTHLY BUDGET

INCOME	BUDGET	ACTUAL	DIFFERENCE	NOTES
SOURCE	$			
SOURCE	$			
TOTAL	$			
SAVINGS				
TOTAL	$			
INVESTING/RETIREMENTS				
	$			
	$			
TOTAL	$			
HOUSING + UTILITIES				
	$			
	$			
	$			
	$			
TOTAL	$			
STUDENT LOANS				
	$			
	$			
TOTAL	$			
TRANSPORTATION				
CAR PAYMENTS	$			
PUBLIC TRANSPORTATION	$			
TAXI	$			
INSURANCE	$			
GAS	$			
TOTAL	$			
FOOD				
GROCERIES	$			
DINING OUT	$			
TOTAL	$			
PERSONAL				
TOILETRIES	$			
BEAUTY (HAIR & NAILS)	$			
OTHER	$			
MEDICAL	$			
TOTAL	$			
CREDIT CARDS				
	$			
	$			
	$			
TOTAL	$			
OTHER EXPENSES				
	$			
	$			
	$			
TOTAL	$			
GRAND TOTAL	$			

DAILY EXPENSE TRACKER

DATE	DESCRIPTION	CATEGORY	AMOUNT	CASH/ CREDIT OR DEBIT?	NEED OR WANT?
			$		
			$		
			$		
			$		
			$		
			$		
			$		
			$		
			$		
			$		
			$		
			$		
			$		
			$		
			$		
			$		
			$		
			$		
			$		
			$		
			$		
			$		
			$		
			$		
		TOTAL	$		

MYFABFINANCE.COM

DEBT REPAYMENT PLAN

COMPANY INFO		ACCOUNT NUMBER	CREDIT TYPE
CREDIT LIMIT	INTEREST RATE	TERM	INTEREST ACCRUED
GOAL PAYOFF DATE	MINIMUM PAYMENT	DUE DATE	STARTING BALANCE
WEBSITE		USERNAME	PASSWORD

BALANCE	PAYMENT AMOUNT	DATE	CURRENT AMOUNT	NOTES

MYFABFINANCE.COM

DEBT REPAYMENT PLAN

COMPANY INFO		ACCOUNT NUMBER	CREDIT TYPE
CREDIT LIMIT	INTEREST RATE	TERM	INTEREST ACCRUED
GOAL PAYOFF DATE	MINIMUM PAYMENT	DUE DATE	STARTING BALANCE
WEBSITE		USERNAME	PASSWORD

BALANCE	PAYMENT AMOUNT	DATE	CURRENT AMOUNT	NOTES

MYFABFINANCE.COM

DEBT REPAYMENT PLAN

COMPANY INFO		ACCOUNT NUMBER	CREDIT TYPE
CREDIT LIMIT	INTEREST RATE	TERM	INTEREST ACCRUED
GOAL PAYOFF DATE	MINIMUM PAYMENT	DUE DATE	STARTING BALANCE
WEBSITE		USERNAME	PASSWORD

BALANCE	PAYMENT AMOUNT	DATE	CURRENT AMOUNT	NOTES

MYFABFINANCE.COM

MONTH 5

> "THE TRUE COST OF ANYTHING IS THE AMOUNT OF LIFE YOU EXCHANGE FOR IT"

MONTHLY CHALLENGE

Wait 24 Hours

Force yourself to wait 24 hours before making any purchase that is not a necessity.

GOALS FOR THIS MONTH:

○

○

○

I'M GRATEFUL FOR

TALK MONEY WITH TONYA

EMERGENCY FUND

An emergency fund is just that, a fund set up to help you handle life's emergencies. So a sample sale or a going out of a business sale is not an emergency. We are all adults here, but for clarification purposes, I will name a few "emergencies": a transportation break down, a home maintenance issue, an unforeseen medical incident, or a job loss.

Emergency funds are set up to help you during the types of occurrences listed above. But just how much do you need to make sure you are prepared? The rule at thumb is that you should have at least 3 months' salary in your emergency fund. For example, if you make $2,500 after taxes you should have $7,500 in your emergency fund.

If that seems like a large amount to you, don't worry. Contribute as much as you reasonably can and consider putting the money in an online account that you don't have access to. One of the quickest ways to let your money grow is to make the account inconvenient.

MYFABFINANCE.COM

FINANCIAL CALENDAR

MONTH OF: _____

MONDAY	TUESDAY	WEDNESDAY	THURSDAY	FRIDAY	SATURDAY	SUNDAY

MONTHLY BUDGET

INCOME	BUDGET	ACTUAL	DIFFERENCE	NOTES
SOURCE	$			
SOURCE	$			
TOTAL	$			
SAVINGS				
TOTAL	$			
INVESTING/RETIREMENTS				
	$			
	$			
TOTAL	$			
HOUSING + UTILITIES				
	$			
	$			
	$			
	$			
TOTAL	$			
STUDENT LOANS				
	$			
	$			
TOTAL	$			
TRANSPORTATION				
CAR PAYMENTS	$			
PUBLIC TRANSPORTATION	$			
TAXI	$			
INSURANCE	$			
GAS	$			
TOTAL	$			
FOOD				
GROCERIES	$			
DINING OUT	$			
TOTAL	$			
PERSONAL				
TOILETRIES	$			
BEAUTY (HAIR & NAILS)	$			
OTHER	$			
MEDICAL	$			
TOTAL	$			
CREDIT CARDS				
	$			
	$			
	$			
TOTAL	$			
OTHER EXPENSES				
	$			
	$			
	$			
TOTAL	$			
GRAND TOTAL	$			

DAILY EXPENSE TRACKER

DATE	DESCRIPTION	CATEGORY	AMOUNT	CASH/ CREDIT OR DEBIT?	NEED OR WANT?
			$		
			$		
			$		
			$		
			$		
			$		
			$		
			$		
			$		
			$		
			$		
			$		
			$		
			$		
			$		
			$		
			$		
			$		
			$		
			$		
			$		
			$		
			$		
			$		
		TOTAL	$		

MYFABFINANCE.COM

MONTH 6

> ## "THE ART IS NOT IN MAKING MONEY, BUT IN KEEPING IT"

MONTHLY CHALLENGE:

Go all Cash

Challenge yourself to use all cash for a pay period. Set a budget for how much you will spend on non-necessities. You can pay your bills online with your card but all other purchases must come out of your pre-allocated cash budget.

And NO visiting the ATM machines once you have taken out your allocated amount.

GOALS FOR THIS MONTH:

- ○
- ○
- ○

I'M GRATEFUL FOR

FINANCIAL CALENDAR

MONDAY	TUESDAY	WEDNESDAY	THURSDAY	FRIDAY	SATURDAY	SUNDAY

MYFABFINANCE.COM

MONTHLY BUDGET

INCOME	BUDGET	ACTUAL	DIFFERENCE	NOTES
SOURCE	$			
SOURCE	$			
TOTAL	$			
SAVINGS				
TOTAL	$			
INVESTING/RETIREMENTS				
	$			
	$			
TOTAL	$			
HOUSING + UTILITIES				
	$			
	$			
	$			
	$			
TOTAL	$			
STUDENT LOANS				
	$			
	$			
TOTAL	$			
TRANSPORTATION				
CAR PAYMENTS	$			
PUBLIC TRANSPORTATION	$			
TAXI	$			
INSURANCE	$			
GAS	$			
TOTAL	$			
FOOD				
GROCERIES	$			
DINING OUT	$			
TOTAL	$			
PERSONAL				
TOILETRIES	$			
BEAUTY (HAIR & NAILS)	$			
OTHER	$			
MEDICAL	$			
TOTAL	$			
CREDIT CARDS				
	$			
	$			
	$			
TOTAL	$			
OTHER EXPENSES				
	$			
	$			
	$			
TOTAL	$			
GRAND TOTAL	$			

DAILY EXPENSE TRACKER

DATE	DESCRIPTION	CATEGORY	AMOUNT	CASH/ CREDIT OR DEBIT?	NEED OR WANT?
			$		
			$		
			$		
			$		
			$		
			$		
			$		
			$		
			$		
			$		
			$		
			$		
			$		
			$		
			$		
			$		
			$		
			$		
			$		
			$		
			$		
			$		
			$		
			$		
		TOTAL	$		

MYFABFINANCE.COM

MONTH 7

"JUST BECAUSE YOU CAN DOESN'T MEAN YOU SHOULD."

MONTHLY CHALLENGE:

Do something yourself.

Learn to do something that you normally pay for yourself such as your hair, manicure, makeup, cocktail mixing, pet grooming, etc.

GOALS FOR THIS MONTH:

○

○

○

I'M GRATEFUL FOR

TALK MONEY WITH TONYA

FINDING A FINANCIAL PROFESSIONAL

If you'd prefer the help of a financial professional to help you begin investing and planning for the future, read on!

First things first, how do you find a financial professional? Ask around. Ask your friends and colleagues if they have anyone that they work with. If you can't find someone through your circle reach out to a non-profit organization, search for an investment club through better investing.org, or consider employing the help of a robo-advisor such as LearnVest.

If you aren't working with a advisor of well-established company, make sure to check for up-to- date certifications and credentials. Be wary of anyone who says that they can outperform the market. Scammers are out there. If it sounds too good to be true then it probably is.

MYFABFINANCE.COM

FINANCIAL CALENDAR

MONDAY	TUESDAY	WEDNESDAY	THURSDAY	FRIDAY	SATURDAY	SUNDAY

MYFABFINANCE.COM

MONTHLY BUDGET

INCOME	BUDGET	ACTUAL	DIFFERENCE	NOTES
SOURCE	$			
SOURCE	$			
TOTAL	$			
SAVINGS				
TOTAL	$			
INVESTING/RETIREMENTS				
	$			
	$			
TOTAL	$			
HOUSING + UTILITIES				
	$			
	$			
	$			
	$			
TOTAL	$			
STUDENT LOANS				
	$			
	$			
TOTAL	$			
TRANSPORTATION				
CAR PAYMENTS	$			
PUBLIC TRANSPORTATION	$			
TAXI	$			
INSURANCE	$			
GAS	$			
TOTAL	$			
FOOD				
GROCERIES	$			
DINING OUT	$			
TOTAL	$			
PERSONAL				
TOILETRIES	$			
BEAUTY (HAIR & NAILS)	$			
OTHER	$			
MEDICAL	$			
TOTAL	$			
CREDIT CARDS				
	$			
	$			
	$			
TOTAL	$			
OTHER EXPENSES				
	$			
	$			
	$			
TOTAL	$			
GRAND TOTAL	$			

DAILY EXPENSE TRACKER

DATE	DESCRIPTION	CATEGORY	AMOUNT	CASH/ CREDIT OR DEBIT?	NEED OR WANT?
			$		
			$		
			$		
			$		
			$		
			$		
			$		
			$		
			$		
			$		
			$		
			$		
			$		
			$		
			$		
			$		
			$		
			$		
			$		
			$		
			$		
			$		
			$		
			$		
		TOTAL	$		

MYFABFINANCE.COM

DEBT REPAYMENT PLAN

COMPANY INFO		ACCOUNT NUMBER	CREDIT TYPE
CREDIT LIMIT	INTEREST RATE	TERM	INTEREST ACCRUED
GOAL PAYOFF DATE	MINIMUM PAYMENT	DUE DATE	STARTING BALANCE
WEBSITE		USERNAME	PASSWORD

BALANCE	PAYMENT AMOUNT	DATE	CURRENT AMOUNT	NOTES

MYFABFINANCE.COM

DEBT REPAYMENT PLAN

COMPANY INFO		ACCOUNT NUMBER	CREDIT TYPE
CREDIT LIMIT	INTEREST RATE	TERM	INTEREST ACCRUED
GOAL PAYOFF DATE	MINIMUM PAYMENT	DUE DATE	STARTING BALANCE
WEBSITE		USERNAME	PASSWORD

BALANCE	PAYMENT AMOUNT	DATE	CURRENT AMOUNT	NOTES

MYFABFINANCE.COM

DEBT REPAYMENT PLAN

COMPANY INFO		ACCOUNT NUMBER	CREDIT TYPE
CREDIT LIMIT	INTEREST RATE	TERM	INTEREST ACCRUED
GOAL PAYOFF DATE	MINIMUM PAYMENT	DUE DATE	STARTING BALANCE
WEBSITE		USERNAME	PASSWORD

BALANCE	PAYMENT AMOUNT	DATE	CURRENT AMOUNT	NOTES

MYFABFINANCE.COM

NETWORTH BALANCE

ASSETS			LIABILITIES		
CASH			**DEBTS**		
		$			$
		$			$
		$			$
		$			$
		$			$
	SUBTOTAL	$		SUBTOTAL	$
REAL ESTATE			**MORTGAGES**		
		$			$
		$			$
		$			$
		$			$
		$			$
	SUBTOTAL	$		SUBTOTAL	$
INVESTMENTS			**LOANS**		
		$			$
		$			$
		$			$
		$			$
		$			$
	SUBTOTAL	$		SUBTOTAL	$
	TOTAL	$		**TOTAL**	$

DATE	TOTAL ASSETS	TOTAL LIABILITY	NETWORTH
FICO SCORE	EQUIFAX	EXPIRIAN	TRANS UNION

MYFABFINANCE.COM

ACCOUNT INFORMATION

COMPANY INFO		ACCOUNT NUMBER
WEBSITE		SECURITY QUESTION
USERNAME	PASSWORD	SECURITY ANSWER
COMPANY INFO		ACCOUNT NUMBER
WEBSITE		SECURITY QUESTION
USERNAME	PASSWORD	SECURITY ANSWER
COMPANY INFO		ACCOUNT NUMBER
WEBSITE		SECURITY QUESTION
USERNAME	PASSWORD	SECURITY ANSWER
COMPANY INFO		ACCOUNT NUMBER
WEBSITE		SECURITY QUESTION
USERNAME	PASSWORD	SECURITY ANSWER
COMPANY INFO		ACCOUNT NUMBER
WEBSITE		SECURITY QUESTION
USERNAME	PASSWORD	SECURITY ANSWER
COMPANY INFO		ACCOUNT NUMBER
WEBSITE		SECURITY QUESTION
USERNAME	PASSWORD	SECURITY ANSWER

MYFABFINANCE.COM

ACCOUNT INFORMATION

COMPANY INFO		ACCOUNT NUMBER
WEBSITE		SECURITY QUESTION
USERNAME	PASSWORD	SECURITY ANSWER
COMPANY INFO		ACCOUNT NUMBER
WEBSITE		SECURITY QUESTION
USERNAME	PASSWORD	SECURITY ANSWER
COMPANY INFO		ACCOUNT NUMBER
WEBSITE		SECURITY QUESTION
USERNAME	PASSWORD	SECURITY ANSWER
COMPANY INFO		ACCOUNT NUMBER
WEBSITE		SECURITY QUESTION
USERNAME	PASSWORD	SECURITY ANSWER
COMPANY INFO		ACCOUNT NUMBER
WEBSITE		SECURITY QUESTION
USERNAME	PASSWORD	SECURITY ANSWER
COMPANY INFO		ACCOUNT NUMBER
WEBSITE		SECURITY QUESTION
USERNAME	PASSWORD	SECURITY ANSWER

MYFABFINANCE.COM

MONTH 8

> *"EARNING MORE USUALLY DOES NOT SOLVE THE PROBLEM. YOU WILL NEVER HAVE ENOUGH IF YOU DO NOT LEARN TO PROPERLY MANAGE WHAT YOU CURRENTLY HAVE"*

MONTHLY CHALLENGE:

Empty your cupboards.

Challenge yourself to reduce trips to the grocery store by making meals using the existing items in your cupboard.

GOALS FOR THIS MONTH:

○

○

○

MYFABFINANCE.COM

I'M GRATEFUL FOR

MONTH OF: _____

FINANCIAL CALENDAR

MONDAY	TUESDAY	WEDNESDAY	THURSDAY	FRIDAY	SATURDAY	SUNDAY

MYFABFINANCE.COM

MONTHLY BUDGET

INCOME	BUDGET	ACTUAL	DIFFERENCE	NOTES
SOURCE	$			
SOURCE	$			
TOTAL	$			
SAVINGS				
TOTAL	$			
INVESTING/RETIREMENTS				
	$			
	$			
TOTAL	$			
HOUSING + UTILITIES				
	$			
	$			
	$			
	$			
TOTAL	$			
STUDENT LOANS				
	$			
	$			
TOTAL	$			
TRANSPORTATION				
CAR PAYMENTS	$			
PUBLIC TRANSPORTATION	$			
TAXI	$			
INSURANCE	$			
GAS	$			
TOTAL	$			
FOOD				
GROCERIES	$			
DINING OUT	$			
TOTAL	$			
PERSONAL				
TOILETRIES	$			
BEAUTY (HAIR & NAILS)	$			
OTHER	$			
MEDICAL	$			
TOTAL	$			
CREDIT CARDS				
	$			
	$			
	$			
TOTAL	$			
OTHER EXPENSES				
	$			
	$			
	$			
TOTAL	$			
GRAND TOTAL	$			

DAILY EXPENSE TRACKER

DATE	DESCRIPTION	CATEGORY	AMOUNT	CASH/ CREDIT OR DEBIT?	NEED OR WANT?
			$		
			$		
			$		
			$		
			$		
			$		
			$		
			$		
			$		
			$		
			$		
			$		
			$		
			$		
			$		
			$		
			$		
			$		
			$		
			$		
			$		
			$		
			$		
			$		
	TOTAL		$		

MYFABFINANCE.COM

MONTH 9

"YOU DON'T HAVE TO BE GREAT TO START, BUT YOU DO HAVE TO START IN ORDER TO BE GREAT."

MONTHLY CHALLENGE:

Pay extra on a bill.

Make room in your budget to pay a little extra towards the principle on one of your installment debts such as your mortgage, student loan, or auto-loan. An additional $50-$200 can go a long way.

GOALS FOR THIS MONTH:

○

○

○

I'M GRATEFUL FOR

TALK MONEY WITH TONYA

LEASING VS. BUYING

I'm often asked whether it's better to buy or lease a new car. While I love the smell of a new car it isn't always the best purchasing decision. As someone who once sold cars for a living I can tell you with certainty that a car's value depreciates when you drive it off of the lot. With this in mind, the decision to lease or buy should be based on your current and future circumstance.

Leasing a car is similar to renting an apartment. The payments are often low, maintenance costs are minimal, and you can exchange the vehicle for a new one after your leasing period ends (usually 24-36 months) without owing more than the vehicle is worth. For these perks, leasing typically requires better credit than buying. The downside of leasing is that there is often a limit on the amount of miles you can drive during the lease period. If you exceed your mileage allowance it can end up costing around $.25 for per extra mile, which can become quite expensive.

Buying a car is like buying a home. You can drive it as much as you please, customize it, and (assuming you pay it off) you can own the vehicle and be debt free. Your prices and payment terms will also be more flexible when buying, so I recommend you choose a financing option that doesn't exceed 60 months. A drawback of buying a car is that once the vehicle is out of warranty, you are responsible for its maintenance.

When buying or leasing a car, it is important to be aware of deals available. It doesn't hurt to bring someone who is knowledgeable about the car buying process and dealer tactics. If that isn't an option, educate yourself before walking onto a car lot. A well-informed buyer is a dealerships worst nightmare!

MYFABFINANCE.COM

FINANCIAL CALENDAR

MONTH OF: _____

MONDAY	TUESDAY	WEDNESDAY	THURSDAY	FRIDAY	SATURDAY	SUNDAY

MONTHLY BUDGET

INCOME	BUDGET	ACTUAL	DIFFERENCE	NOTES
SOURCE	$			
SOURCE	$			
TOTAL	$			
SAVINGS				
TOTAL	$			
INVESTING/RETIREMENTS				
	$			
	$			
TOTAL	$			
HOUSING + UTILITIES				
	$			
	$			
	$			
	$			
TOTAL	$			
STUDENT LOANS				
	$			
	$			
TOTAL	$			
TRANSPORTATION				
CAR PAYMENTS	$			
PUBLIC TRANSPORTATION	$			
TAXI	$			
INSURANCE	$			
GAS	$			
TOTAL	$			
FOOD				
GROCERIES	$			
DINING OUT	$			
TOTAL	$			
PERSONAL				
TOILETRIES	$			
BEAUTY (HAIR & NAILS)	$			
OTHER	$			
MEDICAL	$			
TOTAL	$			
CREDIT CARDS				
	$			
	$			
	$			
TOTAL	$			
OTHER EXPENSES				
	$			
	$			
	$			
TOTAL	$			
GRAND TOTAL	$			

DAILY EXPENSE TRACKER

DATE	DESCRIPTION	CATEGORY	AMOUNT	CASH/ CREDIT OR DEBIT?	NEED OR WANT?
			$		
			$		
			$		
			$		
			$		
			$		
			$		
			$		
			$		
			$		
			$		
			$		
			$		
			$		
			$		
			$		
			$		
			$		
			$		
			$		
			$		
			$		
			$		
			$		
		TOTAL	$		

MYFABFINANCE.COM

MONTH 10

"BE CAREFUL NOT TO COMPARE YOUR SITUATION WITH INDIVIDUALS WHO ARE LIVING IN VIRTUAL PROSPERITY.

MONTHLY CHALLENGE:

Go on a social media fast.

Eliminate Facebook, Instagram, and Twitter for at least 72 hours.

GOALS FOR THIS MONTH:

○

○

○

I'M GRATEFUL FOR

FINANCIAL CALENDAR

MONDAY	TUESDAY	WEDNESDAY	THURSDAY	FRIDAY	SATURDAY	SUNDAY

MYFABFINANCE.COM

MONTHLY BUDGET

INCOME	BUDGET	ACTUAL	DIFFERENCE	NOTES
SOURCE	$			
SOURCE	$			
TOTAL	$			
SAVINGS				
TOTAL	$			
INVESTING/RETIREMENTS				
	$			
	$			
TOTAL	$			
HOUSING + UTILITIES				
	$			
	$			
	$			
	$			
TOTAL	$			
STUDENT LOANS				
	$			
	$			
TOTAL	$			
TRANSPORTATION				
CAR PAYMENTS	$			
PUBLIC TRANSPORTATION	$			
TAXI	$			
INSURANCE	$			
GAS	$			
TOTAL	$			
FOOD				
GROCERIES	$			
DINING OUT	$			
TOTAL	$			
PERSONAL				
TOILETRIES	$			
BEAUTY (HAIR & NAILS)	$			
OTHER	$			
MEDICAL	$			
TOTAL	$			
CREDIT CARDS				
	$			
	$			
	$			
TOTAL	$			
OTHER EXPENSES				
	$			
	$			
	$			
TOTAL	$			
GRAND TOTAL	$			

DAILY EXPENSE TRACKER

DATE	DESCRIPTION	CATEGORY	AMOUNT	CASH/ CREDIT OR DEBIT?	NEED OR WANT?
			$		
			$		
			$		
			$		
			$		
			$		
			$		
			$		
			$		
			$		
			$		
			$		
			$		
			$		
			$		
			$		
			$		
			$		
			$		
			$		
			$		
			$		
			$		
			$		
		TOTAL	$		

MYFABFINANCE.COM

DEBT REPAYMENT PLAN

COMPANY INFO		ACCOUNT NUMBER	CREDIT TYPE
CREDIT LIMIT	INTEREST RATE	TERM	INTEREST ACCRUED
GOAL PAYOFF DATE	MINIMUM PAYMENT	DUE DATE	STARTING BALANCE
WEBSITE		USERNAME	PASSWORD

BALANCE	PAYMENT AMOUNT	DATE	CURRENT AMOUNT	NOTES

MYFABFINANCE.COM

DEBT REPAYMENT PLAN

COMPANY INFO		ACCOUNT NUMBER	CREDIT TYPE
CREDIT LIMIT	INTEREST RATE	TERM	INTEREST ACCRUED
GOAL PAYOFF DATE	MINIMUM PAYMENT	DUE DATE	STARTING BALANCE
WEBSITE		USERNAME	PASSWORD

BALANCE	PAYMENT AMOUNT	DATE	CURRENT AMOUNT	NOTES

MYFABFINANCE.COM

DEBT REPAYMENT PLAN

COMPANY INFO		ACCOUNT NUMBER	CREDIT TYPE
CREDIT LIMIT	INTEREST RATE	TERM	INTEREST ACCRUED
GOAL PAYOFF DATE	MINIMUM PAYMENT	DUE DATE	STARTING BALANCE
WEBSITE		USERNAME	PASSWORD

BALANCE	PAYMENT AMOUNT	DATE	CURRENT AMOUNT	NOTES

MYFABFINANCE.COM

MONTH 11

"TAKE TIME TO REFLECT ON ALL OF THE BLESSINGS YOU HAVE THAT MONEY CAN'T BUY."

MONTHLY CHALLENGE:

Use what you got to make a little extra money.

Sell unused items or clothes in your house.

GOALS FOR THIS MONTH:
- ○
- ○
- ○

I'M GRATEFUL FOR

TALK MONEY WITH TONYA

STARTING A BUSINESS ON A BUDGET

It takes money to make money and that's just the nature of that business. But there are hundreds of thousands of businesses that began with humble beginnings. Do not count yourself out simply because you don't have a major investor. You can make your dream happen without a dream budget.

When starting out on a shoestring budget one of the best things you can do is leverage your existing talents or resources. Think about how the people that are in your life can help you with your business and also about the skills that you possess. When I first started My Fab Finance I bartered credit repair services for everything from social media management to hairstyling.

Lastly...remember that although big aspirations are great, don't be afraid to start small, start local and grow from there.

MONTH OF: _____

FINANCIAL CALENDAR

MONDAY	TUESDAY	WEDNESDAY	THURSDAY	FRIDAY	SATURDAY	SUNDAY

MYFABFINANCE.COM

MONTHLY BUDGET

INCOME	BUDGET	ACTUAL	DIFFERENCE	NOTES
SOURCE	$			
SOURCE	$			
TOTAL	$			
SAVINGS				
TOTAL	$			
INVESTING/RETIREMENTS				
	$			
	$			
TOTAL	$			
HOUSING + UTILITIES				
	$			
	$			
	$			
	$			
TOTAL	$			
STUDENT LOANS				
	$			
	$			
TOTAL	$			
TRANSPORTATION				
CAR PAYMENTS	$			
PUBLIC TRANSPORTATION	$			
TAXI	$			
INSURANCE	$			
GAS	$			
TOTAL	$			
FOOD				
GROCERIES	$			
DINING OUT	$			
TOTAL	$			
PERSONAL				
TOILETRIES	$			
BEAUTY (HAIR & NAILS)	$			
OTHER	$			
MEDICAL	$			
TOTAL	$			
CREDIT CARDS				
	$			
	$			
	$			
TOTAL	$			
OTHER EXPENSES				
	$			
	$			
	$			
TOTAL	$			
GRAND TOTAL	$			

DAILY EXPENSE TRACKER

DATE	DESCRIPTION	CATEGORY	AMOUNT	CASH/ CREDIT OR DEBIT?	NEED OR WANT?
			$		
			$		
			$		
			$		
			$		
			$		
			$		
			$		
			$		
			$		
			$		
			$		
			$		
			$		
			$		
			$		
			$		
			$		
			$		
			$		
			$		
			$		
			$		
			$		
			$		
	TOTAL		$		

MYFABFINANCE.COM

MONTH 12

> # "YOU DON'T NEED ALL OF THE MONEY IN THE WORLD TO MAKE THE WORLD A BETTER PLACE."

MONTHLY CHALLENGE:

Volunteer your time.

Find an organization or a cause you believe in and dedicate at least 5 hours to serving a less fortunate population.

GOALS FOR THIS MONTH:

- ◯
- ◯
- ◯

I'M GRATEFUL FOR

FINANCIAL CALENDAR

MONDAY	TUESDAY	WEDNESDAY	THURSDAY	FRIDAY	SATURDAY	SUNDAY

MYFABFINANCE.COM

MONTHLY BUDGET

INCOME	BUDGET	ACTUAL	DIFFERENCE	NOTES
SOURCE	$			
SOURCE	$			
TOTAL	$			
SAVINGS				
TOTAL	$			
INVESTING/RETIREMENTS				
	$			
	$			
TOTAL	$			
HOUSING + UTILITIES				
	$			
	$			
	$			
	$			
TOTAL	$			
STUDENT LOANS				
	$			
	$			
TOTAL	$			
TRANSPORTATION				
CAR PAYMENTS	$			
PUBLIC TRANSPORTATION	$			
TAXI	$			
INSURANCE	$			
GAS	$			
TOTAL	$			
FOOD				
GROCERIES	$			
DINING OUT	$			
TOTAL	$			
PERSONAL				
TOILETRIES	$			
BEAUTY (HAIR & NAILS)	$			
OTHER	$			
MEDICAL	$			
TOTAL	$			
CREDIT CARDS				
	$			
	$			
	$			
TOTAL	$			
OTHER EXPENSES				
	$			
	$			
	$			
TOTAL	$			
GRAND TOTAL	$			

MONTHLY BUDGET

INCOME	BUDGET	ACTUAL	DIFFERENCE	NOTES
SOURCE	$			
SOURCE	$			
TOTAL	$			
SAVINGS				
TOTAL	$			
INVESTING/RETIREMENTS				
	$			
	$			
TOTAL	$			
HOUSING + UTILITIES				
	$			
	$			
	$			
	$			
TOTAL	$			
STUDENT LOANS				
	$			
	$			
TOTAL	$			
TRANSPORTATION				
CAR PAYMENTS	$			
PUBLIC TRANSPORTATION	$			
TAXI	$			
INSURANCE	$			
GAS	$			
TOTAL	$			
FOOD				
GROCERIES	$			
DINING OUT	$			
TOTAL	$			
PERSONAL				
TOILETRIES	$			
BEAUTY (HAIR & NAILS)	$			
OTHER	$			
MEDICAL	$			
TOTAL	$			
CREDIT CARDS				
	$			
	$			
	$			
TOTAL	$			
OTHER EXPENSES				
	$			
	$			
	$			
TOTAL	$			
GRAND TOTAL	$			

DAILY EXPENSE TRACKER

DATE	DESCRIPTION	CATEGORY	AMOUNT	CASH/ CREDIT OR DEBIT?	NEED OR WANT?
			$		
			$		
			$		
			$		
			$		
			$		
			$		
			$		
			$		
			$		
			$		
			$		
			$		
			$		
			$		
			$		
			$		
			$		
			$		
			$		
			$		
			$		
			$		
			$		
		TOTAL	$		

MYFABFINANCE.COM

CONGRATS

Congratulations on taking critical steps in the direction of your financial freedom by completing the Super Fab Financial Planner.

Make sure you connect with us on social!

- @myfabfinance
- facebook.com/myfabfinance
- @myfabfinance
- myfabfinance
- www.myfabfinance.com

Thank you for allowing us to be a part of your journey.

Made in the USA
Monee, IL
11 August 2022